THINGS YOU SHOULD KNOW: MENTAL HEALTH

Alex Murphy

FOREWORD

Dear Reader,

Welcome to "Things You Should Know: Mental Health," a comprehensive guide to understanding and managing mental well-being. As you embark on this journey, I want to express my sincere gratitude for your interest in this topic. Mental health is a fundamental aspect of our lives, and it's crucial to have access to reliable information and resources.

Throughout this book, you will discover essential knowledge about mental health, including its various aspects, common challenges, effective strategies for self-care, and the importance of seeking professional help when needed. Whether you are seeking to enhance your own mental well-being or support someone you care about, this book provides a valuable foundation for fostering mental health and resilience.

As you delve into the chapters, I encourage you to actively engage with the content, reflect on your own experiences, and apply the insights you gain to your daily life. Remember, mental health is a journey, not a destination, and it requires ongoing attention and care.

I would also appreciate it if you could take a moment to leave a review for this book. Your feedback is invaluable in helping me improve and refine this resource for others. Additionally, I invite you to visit my website, **www.thingsyoushouldknowbooks.com**, where I have a selection of other titles available, covering various other topics. I encourage you to explore my other titles, that look into various aspects of personal development and well-being. I believe that by expanding our knowledge and understanding, we can empower ourselves to live fulfilling and meaningful lives.

Thank you for joining me on this journey of understanding mental health. I wish you all the best in your pursuit of well-being and resilience.

Sincerely,

Alex Murphy

CONTENTS

Psychology

INTRODUCTION

Mental health is as vital as physical health, yet it is often neglected or stigmatised. It encompasses our emotional, psychological, and social well-being, affecting our thoughts, feelings, behaviours, stress management, relationships, and decision-making.

Mental health problems can strike anyone, irrespective of age, gender, race, or socioeconomic status. They can be caused by a variety of factors, including genetics, brain chemistry, life experiences, and trauma.

Mental health problems can be mild or severe, and they can be temporary or chronic. Some common mental health problems include:

- Anxiety disorders
- Depressive disorders
- Bipolar disorder
- Schizophrenia
- Eating disorders
- Post-traumatic stress disorder (PTSD)
- Obsessive-compulsive disorder (OCD)

- Substance use disorders

Despite the prevalence of mental health problems, many people are reluctant to seek help. This may be due to stigma, lack of awareness, or difficulty finding affordable and accessible care.

However, it is important to remember that mental health problems are treatable. With the right support, people with mental health conditions can live full and productive lives.

This book is designed to provide you with an overview of mental health. It will cover topics such as:

- What is mental health?
- Common mental health problems
- Causes of mental health problems
- Treatment for mental health problems
- Self-care for mental health
- Mental health in the workplace

I hope that this book will help you to better understand mental health and to seek help if you need it.

CHAPTER 1: WHAT IS MENTAL HEALTH?

Mental health is a complex concept, and there is no single definition that everyone agrees on. However, the World Health Organization (WHO) provides a helpful definition that is widely accepted:

Mental health is a state of well-being in which people are able to realise their full potential, cope with the normal stresses of life, work productively and fruitfully, and make a positive contribution to their community.

This definition highlights the importance of mental health for both individuals and society as a whole. When people have good mental health, they are better able to live fulfilling lives and contribute to the well-being of others.

Mental health is not just the absence of mental illness. It is a positive state of mind that allows us to live our lives to the fullest.

Here are some of the key components of good mental health:

- Emotional well-being: Feeling happy, sad, angry, or scared are all normal human emotions. However, people with good mental health are able to manage their emotions in a healthy way.

- Psychological well-being: This includes having a positive sense of self, feeling confident, and being able to cope with stress.

- Social well-being: This includes having strong relationships with others, feeling connected to your community, and being able to contribute to society.

Mental health is important for everyone, regardless of age, gender, race, or socioeconomic status. It affects how we think, feel, and behave. It also helps determine how we handle stress, relate to others, and make choices.

Good mental health can help us to:

- Live longer, healthier lives
- Have better relationships
- Be more productive at work
- Cope with stress and adversity
- Enjoy life more fully

When people have poor mental health, they may

experience a variety of symptoms, including:

- Difficulty concentrating
- Changes in appetite or sleep
- Fatigue
- Loss of interest in activities that were once enjoyable
- Feelings of sadness, hopelessness, or worthlessness
- Thoughts of death or suicide

If you are experiencing any of these symptoms, it is important to seek help from a mental health professional. Mental health problems are treatable, and early intervention can lead to better outcomes.

Here are some tips for promoting good mental health:

- Get regular exercise. Exercise releases endorphins, which have mood-boosting effects.
- Eat a healthy diet. Eating nutritious foods gives your body the energy it needs to function properly and can also improve your mood.
- Get enough sleep. When you are well-rested, you are better able to cope with stress and manage your emotions.

- Avoid excessive alcohol and drug use. Alcohol and drugs can worsen mental health problems.

- Practice relaxation techniques. Relaxation techniques, such as yoga and meditation, can help to reduce stress and improve mood.

- Connect with supportive people. Having strong social connections can provide you with emotional support and help you to cope with difficult times.

If you are concerned about your own mental health or the mental health of someone you know, please reach out for help. There are many resources available to support people with mental health problems.

CHAPTER 2: COMMON MENTAL HEALTH PROBLEMS

Mental health conditions are widespread, impacting millions of people globally. They can range from mild to severe, and may be temporary or chronic. Some common mental health problems include:

- Anxiety disorders: Anxiety disorders are a group of mental health conditions that cause excessive worry and fear. People with anxiety disorders may experience a variety of symptoms, including restlessness, fatigue, difficulty concentrating, and muscle tension. Anxiety disorders can be classified into several different subtypes, such as generalized anxiety disorder, panic disorder, social anxiety disorder, and specific phobias.

- Depressive disorders: Depressive disorders are another group of common mental health conditions. They are characterised by persistent feelings of sadness, hopelessness, and loss of interest in activities that were once enjoyable. People with depressive disorders may also experience changes in sleep and appetite, difficulty concentrating, and feelings of worthlessness or guilt.

- Bipolar disorder: Bipolar disorder is a mental health condition that causes extreme mood swings, ranging from mania (a state of high energy and euphoria) to depression. During manic episodes, people with bipolar disorder may experience elation, racing thoughts, and decreased need for sleep. During depressive episodes, they may experience the same symptoms as people with depression.

- Schizophrenia: Schizophrenia is a severe mental health condition that causes abnormalities in thinking, perception, behaviour, and emotion. People with schizophrenia may experience hallucinations, delusions, disorganised thinking and speech, and difficulty relating to others.

- Eating disorders: Eating disorders are mental health conditions that involve abnormal eating habits and a distorted body image. People with eating disorders may experience extreme anxiety about food, weight, or body shape. Anorexia nervosa, bulimia nervosa, and binge eating disorder are among the most prevalent eating disorders.

- Post-traumatic stress disorder (PTSD): PTSD is a mental health condition that can develop after a person experiences or witnesses a traumatic event, such as war, violence, or a natural disaster. People with PTSD may experience flashbacks, nightmares, and anxiety related to the trauma. They may also avoid situations that remind them of the trauma.

- Obsessive-compulsive disorder (OCD): OCD is a mental health condition that causes unwanted and intrusive thoughts (obsessions) and repetitive behaviours or rituals (compulsions) that people feel driven to perform. People with OCD may spend hours performing rituals, such as washing their hands or checking locks, in order to reduce anxiety.

- Substance use disorders: Substance use disorders are mental health conditions characterized by the excessive use of alcohol or drugs to the point where it interferes with a person's life. People with substance use disorders may experience cravings, withdrawal symptoms, and difficulty controlling their use of the substance.

Symptoms of Mental Health Problems

The symptoms of mental health problems can vary depending on the specific disorder. However, some common symptoms include:

- Changes in mood
- Changes in sleep patterns
- Changes in appetite
- Difficulty concentrating or making decisions
- Fatigue or low energy
- Loss of interest in activities that were once enjoyable
- Feelings of worthlessness or hopelessness
- Thoughts of death or suicide

Treatment for Mental Health Problems

Multiple mental health treatments exist, including therapy, medication, or a combination of the two.

- Therapy: Therapy can help people to understand and manage their mental health problems. There are many different types of therapy, including cognitive-behavioural therapy (CBT), interpersonal therapy (IPT), and psychodynamic therapy. CBT is a type of therapy that focuses on helping people to identify and change negative thoughts and beliefs. IPT is a type of therapy that focuses on improving relationships and communication skills. Psychodynamic therapy is a type of therapy that focuses on helping people to understand the unconscious roots of their mental health problems.

- Medication: Medication can help to improve brain chemistry and reduce symptoms of mental health problems. Some common medications used to treat mental health problems include antidepressants, antipsychotics, and mood stabilisers. Antidepressants, antipsychotics, and mood stabilisers are psychotropic medications used to treat mental health disorders such as depression, anxiety, schizophrenia, and bipolar disorder.

Self-Care for Mental Health

In addition to professional treatment, there are a number of things that people can do to take care of their mental health. These include:

- Getting regular exercise
- Eating a healthy diet
- Getting enough sleep
- Avoiding excessive alcohol and drug use

- Practicing relaxation techniques, such as yoga or meditation
- Connecting with supportive friends and family members

Mental health problems are common, but they are treatable. With the right support, people with mental health conditions can live full and meaningful lives. If you are experiencing any of the symptoms of a mental health problem, please reach out to a mental health professional for help.

CHAPTER 3: CAUSES OF MENTAL HEALTH PROBLEMS

The exact causes of mental health problems are not fully understood, but there are a number of factors that may contribute to their development. These factors include:

- Genetics: Mental health problems can run in families, suggesting that there is a genetic component to their development.

- Brain chemistry: Mental health problems are often associated with imbalances in brain chemistry. For example, people with depression may have low levels of serotonin, a neurotransmitter that plays a role in mood regulation.

- Life experiences: Traumatic life events, such as abuse, neglect, or loss, can increase the risk of developing mental health problems.

- Stress: Chronic stress can also contribute to the development of mental health problems.

- Substance abuse: Alcohol and drug use can

worsen the symptoms of mental health problems and make them more difficult to treat.

It is important to note that not everyone who experiences these factors will develop a mental health problem. Mental health problems are complex and there is no single cause. However, understanding the potential risk factors can help people to take steps to protect their mental health.

Here is a more detailed look at some of the specific factors that may contribute to the development of common mental health problems:

- Anxiety disorders: Anxiety disorders are often triggered by stressful life events, such as job loss, relationship problems, or financial difficulties. However, they can also be caused by genetic factors or brain chemistry imbalances.

- Depressive disorders: Depression can be caused by a combination of genetic, biological, and environmental factors. Traumatic life events, such as the death of a loved one or the end of a relationship, can also trigger depression.

- Bipolar disorder: Bipolar disorder is thought to be caused by a combination of genetic and environmental factors. There is a strong genetic component to bipolar disorder, and people who have a family member with the disorder are at an increased risk of developing it themselves.

- Schizophrenia: Schizophrenia is a complex mental health condition that is thought to be caused by a combination of genetic, biological, and environmental factors. Researchers are still working to understand the exact causes of schizophrenia, but it is clear that the disorder is not caused by a single factor.

- Eating disorders: Eating disorders are often triggered by a combination of factors, including genetics, personality traits, and cultural pressures. People with eating disorders may have a distorted body image and may use extreme methods to control their weight, such as restricting food intake, purging, or over exercising.

- Post-traumatic stress disorder (PTSD): PTSD is a mental health condition that can develop after a person experiences or witnesses a traumatic event. Traumatic events can include war, violence, natural disasters, or accidents. People with PTSD may experience flashbacks, nightmares, and anxiety related to the trauma.

- Obsessive-compulsive disorder (OCD): OCD

is a mental health condition that causes unwanted and intrusive thoughts (obsessions) and repetitive behaviours or rituals (compulsions). People with OCD may perform rituals, such as washing their hands or checking locks, in order to reduce anxiety.

- Substance use disorders: Substance use disorders can develop as a way to cope with stress, anxiety, or depression. People with substance use disorders may abuse alcohol, drugs, or other substances to numb their emotions or to feel better.

If you are concerned that you or someone you know may be developing a mental health problem, it is important to seek professional help. A mental health professional can assess the situation and provide appropriate treatment.

CHAPTER 4: TREATMENT FOR MENTAL HEALTH PROBLEMS

There are a variety of treatments available for mental health problems. The best treatment for a particular individual will depend on the specific disorder and the severity of the symptoms.

Some of the most common treatments for mental health problems include:

- Psychotherapy: Psychotherapy, also known as talk therapy, can help people understand and manage their mental health problems. There are many different types of psychotherapy, including cognitive-behavioural therapy (CBT), interpersonal therapy (IPT), and psychodynamic therapy.

- CBT is a type of therapy that focuses on helping people to identify and change negative thoughts and beliefs. For example, a person with anxiety may have the thought that they are going to have a panic attack in a public place. CBT can help the person to identify and challenge this thought and to replace it with a more realistic and helpful thought, such as "I have had panic attacks in the past, but I have always been able to cope with them."

- IPT is a type of therapy that focuses on improving relationships and communication skills. This can be helpful for people with mental health problems, as difficulties in relationships can contribute to their symptoms. For example, a person with depression may withdraw from social activities and avoid spending time with loved ones. IPT can help the person to improve their communication skills and to build stronger relationships.

- Psychodynamic therapy is a type of therapy that focuses on helping people to understand the unconscious roots of their mental health problems. This can be helpful for people with mental health problems that are related to past experiences, such as trauma or abuse. For example, a person with PTSD may have flashbacks to a traumatic event. Psychodynamic therapy can help the person to understand and process these memories and to reduce their impact on their life.

- Medication: Medication can be used to improve brain chemistry and reduce symptoms of mental health problems. Some common medications used to treat mental health problems include antidepressants, antipsychotics, and mood stabilisers.

- Antidepressants are used to treat depression and anxiety disorders. They work by increasing the levels of certain neurotransmitters in the brain, such as serotonin and norepinephrine. These neurotransmitters play a role in mood regulation.
- Antipsychotics are used to treat schizophrenia and other psychotic disorders. They work by blocking the effects of dopamine, a neurotransmitter that is involved in psychosis.

- Mood stabilizers are used to treat bipolar disorder. They work by stabilising mood and preventing mood swings.

- Combined treatment: Many people find that a combination of psychotherapy and medication is the most effective treatment for their mental health problems. Psychotherapy can help people to understand and manage their thoughts and feelings, while medication can help to improve brain chemistry and reduce symptoms.

In addition to formal treatment, there are a number of things that people can do to help themselves manage their mental health problems. These include:

- Getting regular exercise: Exercise releases endorphins, which have mood-boosting effects.

- Eating a healthy diet: Eating a balanced diet provides the body with the nutrients it needs to function properly.

- Getting enough sleep: Sleep is essential for mental and physical health.

- Avoiding excessive alcohol and drug use: Alcohol and drugs can worsen the symptoms of mental health problems and make them more difficult to treat.

- Connecting with supportive friends and family members: Social support can be very helpful for people who are struggling with mental health problems.

If you are struggling with a mental health problem, it is important to know that you are not alone. There are many people who understand what you are going through and who can help you get the treatment and support you need.

Here are some additional tips for getting the most out of treatment:

- Be honest with your therapist about your symptoms and experiences. The more honest you are, the better your therapist will be able to help you.

- Be open to trying different treatment approaches. What works for one person may not work for another. It is important to be patient and willing to try different things until you find what works best for you.

- Take your medication as prescribed. It is important to take your medication as prescribed by your doctor, even if you start to feel better. Stopping medication prematurely can make your symptoms worse.

- Build a support network. Having a support network of friends, family, and other people who understand what you are going through can be very helpful.

Recovery from a mental health problem is possible. With the right treatment and support, you can live a full and meaningful life.

CHAPTER 5: SELF-CARE FOR MENTAL HEALTH

Self-care is important for everyone, but it is especially important for people with mental health problems. Self-care can help people to manage their symptoms, improve their mood, and reduce stress. There are many different ways to practice self-care, and what works for one person may not work for another. It is important to find what works best for you and to make self-care a regular part of your routine.

Here are some tips for self-care for mental health:

- Get regular exercise. Exercise releases endorphins, which have mood-boosting effects. Aim for at least 30 minutes of moderate-intensity exercise most days of the week.

- Eat a healthy diet. Eating a balanced diet provides your body with the nutrients it needs to function properly. Avoid processed foods, sugary drinks, and excessive caffeine and alcohol.

- Get enough sleep. Most adults need 7-8 hours of sleep per night. When you are well-rested, you are better able to cope with stress and manage your symptoms.

- Avoid excessive alcohol and drug use. Alcohol and drugs can worsen the symptoms of mental health problems and make them more difficult to treat.

- Connect with supportive friends and family members. Spending time with loved ones can help to reduce stress and improve mood.

- Practice relaxation techniques. Relaxation techniques such as yoga, meditation, and deep breathing can help to calm the mind and body.

- Do things you enjoy. Make time for activities that you enjoy and that make you feel good. This could include hobbies, spending time with loved ones, or simply relaxing and taking a break.

If you are struggling with a mental health problem, it is important to be patient with yourself. Recovery takes time and effort. But by taking care of yourself and seeking professional help, you can live a full and meaningful life.

Here are some additional tips for self-care for specific mental health problems:

- Anxiety disorders: If you have an anxiety

disorder, it is important to find healthy ways to cope with your anxiety. Some helpful coping mechanisms include relaxation techniques, exercise, and spending time with loved ones. It is also important to avoid caffeine and alcohol, as these substances can worsen anxiety symptoms.

- Depressive disorders: If you have depression, it is important to get regular exercise, eat a healthy diet, and get enough sleep. These things can help to improve your mood and energy levels. It is also important to connect with supportive friends and family members, and to do things that you enjoy.

- Bipolar disorder: If you have bipolar disorder, it is important to follow your treatment plan carefully and to take your medication as prescribed. It is also important to get regular exercise, eat a healthy diet, and get enough sleep. It is also important to avoid caffeine and alcohol, as these substances can trigger mood swings.

- Schizophrenia: If you have schizophrenia, it is important to take your medication as prescribed and to attend your therapy appointments. It is also important to connect with supportive friends and family members, and to do things that you enjoy.

- Eating disorders: If you have an eating disorder, it is important to seek professional help. Eating disorders are complex conditions that require specialized treatment.

- Post-traumatic stress disorder (PTSD): If you have PTSD, it is important to seek professional help. PTSD is a serious condition that can be difficult to treat on your own. A therapist can help you to develop coping mechanisms and to process your trauma.

- Obsessive-compulsive disorder (OCD): If you have OCD, it is important to seek professional help. OCD is a complex condition that requires specialized treatment. A therapist can help you to develop coping mechanisms and to manage your obsessions and compulsions.

- Substance use disorders: If you have a substance use disorder, it is important to seek professional help. Substance use disorders are complex conditions that require specialized treatment. A therapist can help you to understand your addiction and to develop a plan for recovery.

Self-care is an important part of recovery from any mental health problem. By taking care of yourself, you can improve your symptoms, boost your mood, and reduce stress.

CHAPTER 6: MENTAL HEALTH IN THE WORKPLACE

Mental health problems can have a significant impact on people's ability to work. People with mental health problems may experience difficulty concentrating, making decisions, and interacting with others. They may also be more likely to miss work or to leave their jobs altogether.

Employers have a responsibility to create a workplace that is supportive and inclusive of people with mental health problems. This means providing access to mental health resources, creating a stigma-free environment, and accommodating the needs of employees with mental health problems.

Here are some specific things that employers can do to support mental health in the workplace:

- Provide mental health resources. This could include offering employee assistance programs (EAPs), which provide confidential counselling and support services. Employers could also offer workshops or training on mental health awareness and stigma reduction.

- Create a stigma-free environment. This means sending a clear message that mental health problems are real and treatable, and that employees with mental health problems are welcome and supported in the workplace. Employers can do this by talking about mental health openly and honestly, and by promoting a culture of respect and understanding.

- Accommodate the needs of employees with mental health problems. This could involve things like flexible work arrangements, modified work duties, or breaks for mental health breaks. Employers should work with employees to develop individualized accommodations that meet their needs.

When employers take steps to support mental health in the workplace, they benefit as well. Employees who feel supported are more likely to be productive, engaged, and loyal. They are also less likely to miss work or to leave their jobs altogether.

Here are some specific examples of how employers can accommodate the needs of employees with mental health problems:

- An employee with anxiety disorder may need to take breaks throughout the day to de-stress. The employer could allow the employee to work from home on days when they are feeling particularly anxious, or to take short breaks throughout the day to go for a walk or do some deep breathing exercises.

- An employee with depression may need to adjust their work hours to avoid peak times when they are feeling most tired or unmotivated. The employer could allow the employee to start and end work earlier or later, or to take a longer lunch break.

- An employee with bipolar disorder may need to take time off work during manic episodes. The employer could develop a flexible work arrangement that allows the employee to take time off when needed, and to work from home when they are feeling well.

By accommodating the needs of employees with mental health problems, employers can create a more supportive and inclusive workplace for everyone.

CHAPTER 7: MENTAL HEALTH AND RELATIONSHIPS

Mental health can have a significant impact on relationships, both personal and professional. People with mental health problems may experience difficulty communicating, trusting others, and maintaining close relationships. They may also be more likely to experience conflict and relationship breakdown.

However, it is important to remember that mental health problems do not define a person. People with mental health problems can have meaningful and fulfilling relationships. It is possible to build and maintain healthy relationships despite mental health challenges.

Here are some tips for building and maintaining healthy relationships despite mental health challenges:

- Be honest and open with your partner or friends about your mental health condition. This will help them to understand what you are going through and how they can support you.

- Set realistic expectations for yourself and your relationships. It is important to be patient and understanding with yourself and your loved ones.

- Communicate effectively with your partner or friends. Be open about your needs and feelings, and be willing to listen to their concerns.

- Build a support network of people who understand and support you. This could include friends, family members, therapists, or other people with mental health conditions.

Here are some specific challenges that people with mental health problems may face in their relationships:

- Communication difficulties: People with mental health problems may experience difficulty communicating their thoughts and feelings effectively. They may also be more likely to withdraw from social interaction.

- Trust issues: People with mental health problems may have difficulty trusting others due to past experiences of trauma or betrayal.

- Conflict: People with mental health problems may be more likely to experience conflict in their relationships due to mood swings, irritability, or difficulty managing stress.

- Relationship breakdown: People with mental health problems may be more likely to experience relationship breakdown due to the challenges listed above.

If you are struggling to maintain healthy relationships due to your mental health condition, there are a number of things you can do:

- Seek professional help. A therapist can teach you coping mechanisms for managing your mental health condition and communicating effectively in your relationships.

- Join a support group. There are many support groups available for people with mental health conditions and their loved ones. Support groups can provide a safe space to share experiences and learn from others.

- Educate yourself about mental health. The more you know about mental health, the better equipped you will be to manage your condition and build healthy relationships.

By taking these steps, you can improve your communication skills, build trust, and manage conflict more effectively. This can help you to build and maintain healthy relationships despite your mental health challenges.

CHAPTER 8: MENTAL HEALTH AND RESILIENCE

Resilience is the capacity to overcome and bounce back from difficult experiences, setbacks, and challenges. It is not an innate trait, but a skill that can be learned and strengthened over time.

Mental health and resilience are closely linked. People with strong resilience are better able to cope with mental health challenges. They are also better able to recover from mental health problems.

There are a number of things that people can do to develop resilience. These include:

- Developing a positive outlook. People with a positive outlook are more likely to see challenges as opportunities for growth and learning. They are also more likely to believe in their ability to overcome challenges.

- Building a strong support network. Having a strong support network of friends, family, and other people who care about you can help you to cope with challenges and setbacks.

- Practicing healthy coping mechanisms. Healthy coping mechanisms can help you to manage stress and deal with difficult emotions. Examples of healthy coping mechanisms include exercise, relaxation techniques, and spending time with loved ones.

- Learning from your experiences. Everyone experiences challenges and setbacks in life. By reflecting on your past experiences and identifying what went well and what could be improved, you can develop the skills and knowledge necessary to navigate future challenges.

Here are some specific ways to develop resilience in the context of mental health problems:

- Educate yourself about your mental health condition. The more knowledge you have about your condition, the better equipped you will be to manage it.

- Develop a treatment plan that works for you. This may involve working with a therapist, taking medication, or making lifestyle changes.

- Set realistic goals for yourself. Instead of

trying to change everything at once, set small, achievable goals for yourself.

- Be patient and kind to yourself. Recovery from a mental health problem takes time. Mental health recovery is a journey, not a destination. Don't be discouraged if you don't see progress right away.

By developing resilience, you can improve your ability to cope with mental health challenges and live a fulfilling life.

Here are some examples of how people with mental health problems have used resilience to overcome challenges:

- A person with depression may develop resilience by setting small, achievable goals for themselves, such as getting out of bed in the morning or going for a short walk.

- A person with anxiety disorder may develop resilience by learning relaxation techniques, such as deep breathing or meditation.

- A person with bipolar disorder may develop resilience by building a strong support network of friends and family members who can help them during manic and depressive episodes.

- A person with schizophrenia may develop

resilience by learning to manage their symptoms and by developing coping mechanisms for dealing with hallucinations and delusions.

By developing resilience, people with mental health problems can live full and meaningful lives.

CHAPTER 9: MENTAL HEALTH ADVOCACY

Mental health advocacy is the process of speaking out and taking action to improve mental health care and services. Mental health advocates work to raise awareness of mental health issues, reduce stigma, and promote mental well-being for all.

There are many ways to get involved in mental health advocacy. Some people choose to advocate on a personal level, by sharing their own experiences with mental illness and advocating for themselves and others. Others choose to advocate on a more public level, by working with organisations to raise awareness of mental health issues, lobby for policy changes, and promote mental health education.

Here are some specific ways to get involved in mental health advocacy:

- Share your story. Talking about your own experiences with mental illness can help to break down stigma and raise awareness of mental health issues. You can share your story through personal essays, social media, or public speaking engagements.

- Volunteer for a mental health organisation. There are many mental health organisations that need volunteers to help with a variety of tasks, such as providing support to people with mental illness, advocating for policy changes, and raising awareness of mental health issues. Some examples of mental health organisations in the UK include:
  - Mind
  - Rethink Mental Illness
  - Sane
  - Time to Change
  - Samaritans
- Contact your MP. Let your MP know that mental health is important to you and that you want them to support policies that improve mental health care and services.
- Donate to mental health charities. There are many charities that are working to improve mental health care and services. Your donation can help to support their important work.

Mental health advocacy is essential for improving the lives of people with mental illness and their families. By getting involved in mental health advocacy, you can help to create a world where everyone has access to the care and support they need.

Here are some examples of successful mental health advocacy campaigns in the UK:

- Mind's Time to Change campaign has been working to reduce stigma associated with mental illness since 2009. The campaign has helped to change public attitudes towards mental illness and has encouraged people to talk about their mental health.

- Rethink Mental Illness's No Time to Lose campaign is working to improve mental health services for young people. The campaign is calling for more mental health professionals to be trained and for better access to mental health services for young people.

- Sane's See the Real Me campaign is working to reduce stigma associated with psychosis. The campaign is challenging stereotypes about people with psychosis and is encouraging people to talk about their experiences.

These are just a few examples of the many successful mental health advocacy campaigns that have been conducted in the UK in recent years. Mental health advocates are making a real difference in the lives of people with mental illness and their families.

If you are interested in getting involved in mental health advocacy, there are many resources available to help you get started. You can find information on mental health advocacy organisations, campaigns, and resources on the websites of Mind, Rethink Mental Illness, Sane, Time to Change, and Samaritans.

CHAPTER 10: MENTAL HEALTH AND SLEEP

Sleep, an essential aspect of human existence, plays a pivotal role in maintaining mental health. During the restorative process of sleep, our brains consolidate memories, process emotions, and rejuvenate themselves, preparing us for the challenges and demands of the waking world. However, the relationship between sleep and mental health is not a one-way street; sleep disturbances can also exacerbate mental health conditions, creating a tangled web of interconnectedness that can be challenging to unravel.

The Impact of Sleep Deprivation on Mental Health

Insufficient sleep can have a profound and detrimental impact on our mental well-being. When we deprive ourselves of the restorative power of sleep, our brains are unable to function optimally, leading to a cascade of negative consequences that can significantly impair our mental health. These consequences include:

- Increased irritability and mood swings: Sleep deprivation can make us more prone to emotional outbursts, heightened sensitivity, and irritability, disrupting our emotional equilibrium.

- Difficulty concentrating and making decisions: Sleep-deprived brains struggle to focus, leading to impaired cognitive function and decision-making abilities. Our ability to process information, prioritize tasks, and make sound judgments diminishes, impacting our daily lives and professional endeavours.

- Heightened anxiety and stress: Sleep deprivation can amplify our stress response, making us more susceptible to anxious thoughts, feelings of apprehension, and a heightened state of vigilance. This can lead to rumination, worry, and an increased risk of panic attacks.

- Increased risk of depression: Studies have shown a strong link between sleep disturbances and the development of depression. Sleep deprivation can contribute to a persistent low mood, anhedonia (loss of pleasure), fatigue, and difficulty concentrating, all of which are hallmark symptoms of depression.

- Impaired emotional regulation: Sleep deprivation can make it difficult to manage our emotions effectively, leading to impulsive behaviour and heightened emotional reactivity. Our ability to self-regulate, control our impulses, and respond appropriately to emotional cues diminishes, potentially leading to strained relationships and interpersonal conflicts.

Sleep Disorders and Their Association with Mental Health Conditions

Specific sleep disorders, such as insomnia and sleep apnoea, can also have a significant and detrimental impact on mental health. These disorders can disrupt sleep patterns, interfere with restorative sleep processes, and exacerbate mental health conditions.

- Insomnia: Insomnia, characterized by difficulty falling or staying asleep, is associated with an increased risk of anxiety, depression, and suicidal ideation. The frustration and distress associated with sleeplessness can amplify anxious thoughts, contribute to persistent sadness, and increase the risk of self-harm or suicidal ideation.

- Sleep apnoea: Sleep apnoea, a condition marked by pauses in breathing during sleep, can lead to daytime fatigue, impaired cognitive function, and increased irritability, which can further contribute to mental health issues. Sleep apnoea can also lead to sleep fragmentation, disrupting the restorative processes of sleep and exacerbating existing mental health conditions.

Strategies for Improving Sleep Habits and Promoting Mental Well-being

Given the bidirectional relationship between sleep and mental health, improving sleep habits can have a positive and transformative impact on our overall well-being. By prioritising sleep and adopting healthy sleep practices, we can enhance our mental health, improve our mood, and increase our resilience in the face of life's challenges. Here are some effective strategies to promote better sleep:

- Establish a regular sleep schedule: Going to bed and waking up at consistent times, even on weekends, helps regulate your body's natural sleep-wake cycle, also known as the circadian rhythm. This consistency helps to signal to your body when it's time to sleep and when it's time to wake up, promoting better sleep quality and reducing daytime fatigue.

- Create a relaxing bedtime routine: Wind down before bed by engaging in calming activities such as reading, taking a warm bath, or listening to soothing music. This helps to transition your mind and body into a state of relaxation, preparing you for sleep. Avoid stimulating activities such as watching TV or working on the computer close to bedtime, as these can interfere with sleep.

- Optimise your sleep environment: Ensure your bedroom is dark, quiet, and cool to promote restful sleep. Darkness encourages the production of melatonin, a hormone that regulates sleep-wake cycles. A quiet environment minimizes distractions and allows for undisturbed sleep. A cool temperature around 18 degrees Celsius is considered ideal for sleep.

- Avoid caffeine and alcohol before bed: Caffeine and alcohol can interfere with sleep, so avoid consuming them close to bedtime. Caffeine is a stimulant that can keep you awake, while alcohol may initially make you drowsy but can disrupt sleep later in the night.

- Get regular exercise: Regular physical activity can improve sleep quality, but avoid strenuous exercise too close to bedtime. Exercise can help to promote better sleep by reducing stress, improving mood, and regulating your body's natural sleep-wake pattern.

- Manage stress effectively: Stress can disrupt sleep patterns, so find healthy ways to manage stress, such as yoga, meditation, or spending time in nature. Relaxation techniques can help to calm your mind and body, making it easier to fall asleep and sleep through the night.

Seek professional help if needed: If you struggle with persistent sleep problems, consult a healthcare professional to rule out underlying medical conditions and receive appropriate treatment. They may recommend cognitive behavioural therapy for insomnia (CBT-I), a type of therapy that can help you change your thoughts and behaviours to promote better sleep. They may also prescribe medication to help you fall asleep or stay asleep.

The relationship between sleep and mental health is complex and multifaceted. Sleep deprivation can exacerbate mental health conditions, while improving sleep habits can promote mental well-being. By prioritising sleep and adopting healthy sleep practices, we can enhance our mental health and overall quality of life.

CHAPTER 11: MENTAL HEALTH AND NUTRITION

The intricate relationship between mental health and nutrition is a subject of ongoing research and exploration. While it is not possible to definitively claim that food can cure mental health conditions, a growing body of evidence suggests that a healthy diet plays a significant role in promoting mental well-being and supporting treatment efforts. By understanding the impact of nutrition on mental health and adopting mindful dietary practices, individuals can empower themselves to enhance their overall health and well-being.

The Impact of Nutrition on Mental Health

The brain, a complex and dynamic organ, requires a variety of essential nutrients to function optimally. When we deprive our brains of these vital nutrients, our mental health can suffer, leading to a range of potential mental health challenges, including:

- Depression: Studies have indicated that individuals with depression may have deficiencies in certain nutrients, such as omega-3 fatty acids, vitamin D, and folate. These nutrients play crucial roles in regulating mood, neurotransmitter activity, and brain cell health.

- Anxiety: A diet rich in processed foods, sugary drinks, and excessive caffeine can exacerbate anxiety symptoms. These substances can contribute to energy crashes, mood swings, and increased alertness, further intensifying anxiety levels.

- Stress: A balanced and wholesome diet can aid in managing stress levels by providing the necessary nutrients for the body to cope with stress hormones. Nutrients like B vitamins, magnesium, and zinc support adrenal gland function and stress resilience.

- Cognitive Decline: A diet rich in fruits, vegetables, and whole grains can help protect against cognitive decline and dementia. These nutrient-dense foods contain antioxidants, anti-inflammatory compounds, and brain-boosting nutrients that support cognitive function and memory.

Nutritional Strategies for Mental Health

By incorporating mindful dietary practices into our

daily lives, we can actively promote mental well-being and support our mental health journey. Here are some key nutritional strategies to consider:

- Embrace Fruits and Vegetables: Fruits and vegetables are nutritional powerhouses, packed with essential vitamins, minerals, and phytonutrients that support brain health and overall well-being. Aim to consume at least five servings of fruits and vegetables daily to reap their benefits.

- Prioritize Whole Grains: Whole grains offer a wealth of nutrients, including fibre, B vitamins, and complex carbohydrates, which provide sustained energy and support brain function. Replace refined grains with whole-grain alternatives like brown rice, quinoa, and whole-wheat bread.

- Incorporate Healthy Fats: Healthy fats, particularly omega-3 fatty acids found in fish like salmon, sardines, and mackerel, play a vital role in brain health and neurotransmitter function. Include healthy fats in your diet by consuming fish, nuts, seeds, and avocado.

- Limit Processed Foods: Processed foods, often high in sugar, unhealthy fats, and sodium, can negatively impact mental health. Minimize consumption of processed snacks, sugary drinks, and fast food to promote a healthier overall diet.

- Stay Hydrated: Dehydration can affect mood, concentration, and energy levels. Make sure to drink plenty of water throughout the day to stay hydrated and support optimal brain function.

Mental Health and Nutrition: A Two-Way Street

The relationship between mental health and nutrition is not merely one-sided; it is a complex and dynamic interplay. While our diet can significantly impact our mental well-being, our mental health can also influence our eating habits. When we experience stress, anxiety, or depression, we may resort to unhealthy food choices as a coping mechanism. This can create a vicious cycle, as poor nutrition can further exacerbate mental health challenges.

Seeking Professional Help

If you are concerned about your mental health, seeking professional help from a qualified mental health professional is crucial. They can assess your individual needs, provide a personalized treatment plan, and offer guidance on nutritional strategies to support your mental health journey.

Remember, you are not alone. Mental health conditions are prevalent, and effective treatments are available. With the right support and mindful self-care practices, you can manage your mental health and live a fulfilling life.

CHAPTER 12: MENTAL HEALTH AND EXERCISE

The benefits of exercise extend far beyond physical fitness and athletic performance. Regular physical activity has been shown to have a profound impact on mental health, offering a range of benefits that can help alleviate stress, improve mood, and enhance overall well-being.

Understanding the Link Between Exercise and Mental Health

The positive effects of exercise on mental health are attributed to a combination of physiological and psychological factors. During exercise, the body releases endorphins, natural painkillers that have mood-boosting effects. Exercise also increases blood flow to the brain, delivering oxygen and nutrients that support cognitive function and mental clarity.

In addition to these physiological effects, exercise can also have a positive impact on mental health by:

- Reducing stress and anxiety: Exercise provides a healthy outlet for pent-up emotions and tension, helping to alleviate stress and anxiety. Physical activity can help to lower stress hormones such as cortisol, and promote the release of stress-reducing endorphins.

- Improving mood and reducing symptoms of depression: Exercise can boost mood and alleviate symptoms of depression by increasing serotonin and norepinephrine, neurotransmitters involved in mood regulation. Exercise can also provide a sense of accomplishment and self-efficacy, which can contribute to improved mood and reduced depressive symptoms.

- Enhancing self-esteem and confidence: Regular physical activity can improve self-esteem and body image, leading to increased confidence and a more positive self-perception. Exercise can help individuals feel more in control of their bodies and their lives, which can boost self-esteem and confidence.

- Promoting better sleep: Exercise can improve sleep quality, which in turn contributes to better mental health and overall well-being. Physical activity can help to tire the body and promote relaxation, making it easier to fall asleep and stay asleep.

Incorporating Exercise into Your Mental Health Routine

The good news is that you don't need to become a marathon runner or gym rat to reap the mental health benefits of exercise. Even moderate-intensity exercise, such as brisk walking, swimming, or cycling, can make a significant difference.

Here are some tips for incorporating exercise into your routine for mental health:

- Find activities you enjoy: Choose activities that you find fun and engaging, rather than forcing yourself to do something you dread. If you enjoy exercise, you are more likely to stick with it in the long run.

- Start small and gradually increase intensity: Begin with shorter durations and gradually increase the amount of time you spend exercising. This will help to prevent injury and make it easier to stick with your routine.

- Make it a habit: Schedule time for exercise in your daily or weekly routine, just like you would any other important appointment. Treat exercise as an important part of your self-care routine.

- Find an exercise buddy: Exercising with a friend or joining a group class can provide motivation and support. Having someone to exercise with can make it more enjoyable and help you to stay accountable.

- Be patient and consistent: It takes time to see noticeable changes in your mental health from exercise. Be patient and consistent with your efforts, and you will start to reap the rewards. Remember, consistency is key to achieving long-term benefits.

Additional Considerations

In addition to the tips mentioned above, here are some additional considerations for incorporating exercise into your mental health routine:

- Listen to your body: Pay attention to your body's signals and avoid overexertion. If you are feeling pain or discomfort, stop the activity and rest.

- Set realistic goals: Set achievable goals that you can gradually build upon. This will help you to stay motivated and avoid feeling overwhelmed.

- Reward yourself: Celebrate your accomplishments and reward yourself for reaching your goals. This will help you to stay motivated and maintain a positive attitude.

Exercise is a powerful tool for improving mental health. By incorporating regular physical activity into your life, you can reduce stress, improve mood, boost self-esteem, and sleep better. Exercise is a safe and effective way to enhance your overall well-being and take charge of your mental health.

CHAPTER 13: MENTAL HEALTH AND MINDFULNESS

In the midst of our fast-paced, technology-driven world, it is easy to become overwhelmed by stress, anxiety, and negative thoughts. Mindfulness, a simple yet profound practice rooted in present-moment awareness, offers a powerful antidote to these challenges. By cultivating mindfulness, we can cultivate a deeper connection with ourselves, our surroundings, and the present moment, leading to significant improvements in our mental well-being.

Understanding Mindfulness

Mindfulness is the practice of paying attention to the present moment without judgment. It involves observing our thoughts, feelings, and sensations without getting caught up in them. This non-judgmental observation allows us to step back from our habitual patterns of thinking and reacting, enabling us to respond to situations with greater clarity and compassion.

Benefits of Mindfulness for Mental Health

Mindfulness has been shown to offer a wide range of

benefits for mental health, including:

- Reduced stress and anxiety: Mindfulness helps us to manage stress and anxiety by shifting our focus away from worry and rumination and towards the present moment. By anchoring ourselves in the present, we can create space between our thoughts and emotions, reducing their intensity and allowing us to respond more effectively.

- Improved sleep: Mindfulness can significantly enhance sleep quality by calming the mind and body, promoting relaxation, and reducing racing thoughts that often interfere with sleep. Mindfulness practices, such as mindful breathing or body scans, can effectively induce relaxation and prepare the mind for restful sleep.

- Increased concentration: Mindfulness cultivates the ability to focus and direct our attention, leading to improved concentration and cognitive function. By training our minds to stay present and avoid distractions, we can enhance our ability to engage fully in tasks, absorb information, and maintain focus.

- Improved mood: Mindfulness can foster a

more positive and balanced outlook by helping us to appreciate the good things in life and cultivate gratitude. By shifting our focus away from negative thoughts and focusing on the present moment, we can cultivate a more positive mindset and enhance our overall mood.

- Reduced reactivity: Mindfulness encourages us to pause and reflect before acting, reducing impulsive or reactive behaviours. By observing our thoughts and emotions without judgment, we can gain a deeper understanding of our triggers and responses, allowing us to make more conscious and compassionate choices.

Incorporating Mindfulness into Daily Life

Mindfulness can be easily integrated into daily life, making it an accessible and practical tool for improving mental health. Here are a few simple ways to incorporate mindfulness into your routine:

- Meditation: Meditation is a cornerstone of mindfulness practice. There are various meditation techniques, including focused-attention meditation, open-monitoring meditation, and loving-kindness meditation. Find a meditation technique that resonates with you and incorporate it into your daily routine, even if it's just for a few minutes each day.

- Mindful breathing: Mindful breathing is a simple yet effective way to cultivate present-moment awareness. Pay attention to the natural rhythm of your breath, noticing the rise and fall of your chest and the sensation of air entering and leaving your nostrils. If your mind wanders, gently guide it back to your breath without judgment.

- Mindful walking: Transform your daily walks into mindfulness exercises. As you walk, focus on the sensations in your body, the feeling of your feet on the ground, and the movement of your muscles. Notice the sights, sounds, and smells around you without getting caught up in thoughts or judgments.

- Mindful eating: Engage with your food mindfully during meals. Take time to savour the flavours, textures, and aromas of your food. Notice the sensations of chewing and swallowing, and appreciate the nourishment your body receives.

- Mindful moments: Throughout the day, take brief pauses to bring your attention to the present moment. Notice your surroundings, your breath, or the sensations in your body. These mindful moments can help you to break out of autopilot and reconnect with yourself and the present.

Tips for Enhancing Mindfulness Practice

As you embark on your mindfulness journey, consider these helpful tips:

- Set aside dedicated time for mindfulness practice. Even a few minutes each day can make a significant difference.

- Be patient with yourself. Developing mindfulness skills takes time and practice. Don't be discouraged if your mind wanders; simply acknowledge it and gently guide your attention back to the present.

- Embrace non-judgmental awareness. Observe your thoughts and emotions without judgment or criticism. Allow them to come and go without getting attached to them.

- Find a supportive environment. If you find it challenging to practice mindfulness on your own, consider joining a mindfulness group or class. The support and guidance of others can enhance your practice.

- Be kind to yourself. Mindfulness is a journey of self-discovery and self-compassion. Be patient with yourself, celebrate your progress, and enjoy the ride.

Mindfulness offers a powerful and transformative approach to enhancing mental well-being. By cultivating present-moment awareness, we can navigate the challenges of daily life with greater clarity, resilience, and compassion. Mindfulness practices can be easily integrated into our daily routines, making it accessible and practical for everyone. As we embark on our mindfulness journey, we invite you to embrace the transformative power of present-moment awareness and discover the profound impact it can have on your mental health and overall well-being.

CHAPTER 14: MENTAL HEALTH AND SOCIAL CONNECTION

Humans are social creatures. We thrive on connection with others, and our relationships play a vital role in our mental and emotional well-being. Strong social connections can buffer us against stress, anxiety, and depression. They can also boost our self-esteem, help us cope with difficult times, and make us feel more connected to our community and the world around us.

The Benefits of Social Connection for Mental Health

Reduced stress and anxiety: Social interaction can help to reduce stress hormones and promote relaxation.

- Improved mood: Spending time with others can boost our mood and make us feel happier.

- Increased self-esteem: Strong social connections can help us to feel more valued and accepted.

- Improved coping skills: Our friends and

family can provide us with support and guidance when we are going through difficult times.

- Reduced risk of depression: Loneliness is a major risk factor for depression. Having strong social connections can help to protect us from this condition.

- Increased physical health: Social connection can also have positive effects on our physical health. For example, studies have shown that people with strong social ties have a lower risk of heart disease, stroke, and dementia.

How to Build Strong Social Connections

There are many things you can do to build strong social connections. Here are a few ideas:

- Join a club or group: There are many clubs and groups available for people of all interests. Joining a club or group is a great way to meet people who share your interests.

- Volunteer: Volunteering is a great way to give back to your community and meet new people.

- Attend social events: Make an effort to attend social events, such as parties, concerts, or sporting events.

- Talk to your neighbours: Get to know your

neighbours by chatting with them when you see them outside.

- Connect with old friends: Reconnect with old friends from school, work, or your neighbourhood.

- Use social media: Social media can be a great way to stay connected with friends and family who live far away.

Tips for Nurturing Your Social Connections

Once you have made some social connections, it is important to nurture them. Here are a few tips:

- Make time for your friends and family: Make time for the people who are important to you, even if you are busy.

- Be a good listener: Show your friends and family that you care about them by listening to them and being supportive.

- Be present: When you are spending time with your friends and family, be present in the moment and avoid distractions, such as your phone.

- Be yourself: Don't try to be someone you're not in order to impress your friends and family.

- Be respectful: Treat your friends and family

with respect, even when you disagree with them.

Social connection is essential for our mental and emotional well-being. By taking steps to build and nurture strong social connections, we can improve our mental health and overall well-being.

CHAPTER 15: MENTAL HEALTH AND POSITIVE PSYCHOLOGY

In the realm of mental health, the traditional focus has often been on alleviating symptoms of distress and pathology. While this approach is essential in addressing mental health challenges, it is equally important to cultivate positive emotions, strengths, and resilience to promote well-being and flourishing. Positive psychology, a relatively new branch of psychology, emerged with the aim of understanding and fostering the conditions that allow individuals and communities to thrive.

Principles of Positive Psychology and Its Applications for Mental Health

Positive psychology is grounded in the belief that humans have an innate capacity for happiness, fulfilment, and positive growth. It challenges the traditional view of mental health as merely the absence of mental illness and instead emphasises the importance of nurturing positive aspects of life.

Key principles of positive psychology include:

- Focus on strengths and resources: Positive psychology encourages individuals to identify and build upon their strengths, talents, and positive qualities rather than solely focusing on deficits and weaknesses.

- Cultivation of positive emotions: Positive emotions, such as joy, gratitude, love, and hope, are seen as essential components of well-being. Positive psychology provides strategies for increasing positive emotions and integrating them into daily life.

- Promotion of resilience and coping skills: Positive psychology emphasizes the importance of resilience, the ability to bounce back from adversity and challenges. It provides strategies for building resilience and developing effective coping mechanisms.

- Encouragement of meaningful goals and purpose: Positive psychology highlights the significance of having meaningful goals and a sense of purpose in life. It helps individuals identify and pursue goals that align with their values and contribute to their overall well-being.

Strategies for Cultivating Positive Emotions, Strengths, and Resilience

Positive psychology offers a variety of practical strategies for cultivating positive emotions, strengths, and resilience:

- Gratitude practice: Regularly expressing gratitude for the good things in life, both big and small, can significantly boost positive emotions and overall well-being.

- Optimism cultivation: Adopting an optimistic outlook and focusing on the positive aspects of life can enhance mood, resilience, and overall well-being.

- Savouring moments of joy: Taking time to savour and appreciate joyful experiences can increase their intensity and duration, leading to greater happiness and well-being.

- Strength's identification and utilisation: Identifying and using one's strengths in various aspects of life can boost confidence, self-esteem, and overall well-being.

- Meaningful goal setting: Setting and pursuing goals that are aligned with one's values and passions can provide a sense of purpose, direction, and fulfilment.

- Mindfulness practice: Engaging in

mindfulness exercises, such as meditation or mindful breathing, can reduce stress, increase focus, and enhance emotional regulation.

- Social connection and support: Building strong social connections and fostering supportive relationships can contribute to happiness, resilience, and overall well-being.

- Acts of kindness: Performing acts of kindness for others can boost positive emotions, enhance self-esteem, and strengthen relationships.

- Self-care and healthy habits: Prioritising self-care practices, such as adequate sleep, nutritious eating, and regular exercise, can promote physical and mental well-being, providing a foundation for positive emotions and resilience.

The Importance of Gratitude, Optimism, and Purpose in Promoting Mental Health

Gratitude, optimism, and purpose play crucial roles in promoting mental health:

- Gratitude: Expressing gratitude shifts our focus from lack and deprivation to abundance and appreciation, fostering a more positive outlook and enhancing happiness.

- Optimism: Maintaining an optimistic mindset cultivates hope, resilience, and a belief in positive outcomes, enabling individuals to approach challenges with a more positive and constructive attitude.

- Purpose: Having a sense of purpose provides direction, meaning, and motivation in life, contributing to overall well-being and mental health.

By incorporating gratitude, optimism, and purpose into our daily lives, we can significantly enhance our mental health and cultivate a more fulfilling and positive existence.

CHAPTER 16: MENTAL HEALTH AND HOPE

In the face of adversity and challenges, hope emerges as a beacon of light, illuminating the path towards recovery and resilience. Hope is the belief that a positive outcome is possible, even in the midst of difficult circumstances. It is the driving force that motivates us to persevere, to reach for better days, and to embrace the possibility of change.

In the context of mental health, hope plays a crucial role in fostering well-being and promoting recovery from mental illness. It is the foundation upon which we build resilience, navigate setbacks, and maintain a positive outlook on life. When hope is present, we are more likely to engage in self-care practices, seek professional help, and maintain a strong support network.

The Power of Hope in Mental Health

Hope is not merely wishful thinking; it is a dynamic force that actively shapes our experiences and behaviours. It empowers us to take action, make decisions, and pursue goals that align with our well-being. By nurturing hope, we cultivate a sense of agency, believing that we have the power to influence our own lives and the course of our mental health journey.

Hope manifests in various forms, and its expression can be unique to each individual. For some, hope may be found in the simple pleasures of life, the beauty of nature, or the kindness of others. For others, hope may reside in the pursuit of personal growth, the striving for meaningful goals, or the belief in a brighter future.

Cultivating Hope in the Face of Mental Health Challenges

Nurturing hope in the face of mental health challenges requires a conscious effort and a commitment to self-care. Here are some strategies to cultivate hope in your mental health journey:

1. Acknowledge your strengths and accomplishments: Take time to reflect on your achievements, no matter how small they may seem. Recognising your strengths and celebrating your successes can boost your self-esteem and reinforce your belief in your ability to overcome challenges.

2. Connect with supportive individuals: Surround yourself with people who genuinely care about your well-being and offer encouragement. A strong support

network can provide solace, understanding, and a sense of belonging, which can significantly enhance your hope and resilience.

3. Engage in activities that bring you joy: Make time for activities that spark joy, creativity, and a sense of fulfilment. Engaging in activities that you enjoy can lift your mood, reduce stress, and foster a positive outlook.

4. Practice mindfulness: Mindfulness techniques, such as meditation or deep breathing exercises, can help you focus on the present moment, reducing anxiety and promoting a sense of calm. Mindfulness can also enhance your ability to appreciate the positive aspects of life, fostering hope and gratitude.

5. Seek professional help when needed: If you are struggling with mental health challenges, seeking professional help from a therapist or counsellor can provide you with the guidance, support, and tools you need to manage your symptoms and cultivate hope for recovery.

Remember, hope is not a fleeting emotion; it is a renewable resource that can be nurtured and strengthened throughout your mental health journey.

By embracing hope, you empower yourself to navigate challenges, pursue personal growth, and cultivate a life filled with meaning and well-being.

CHAPTER 17: THE FUTURE OF MENTAL HEALTH

The future of mental health is bright. With advances in research and treatment, people with mental health conditions are living longer and healthier lives. There is also a growing awareness of the importance of mental health and well-being, which is leading to greater acceptance and support for people with mental health conditions.

Here are some specific trends and developments in the future of mental health:

- Telepsychiatry: Telepsychiatry is the use of technology to provide mental health services remotely. This can be done through video conferencing, phone calls, or even text messaging. Telepsychiatry is making mental health services more accessible and affordable for people in rural areas and for people with mobility challenges.

- Personalised medicine: Personalised medicine is an approach to medicine that takes into account individual genetic and environmental factors to develop tailored treatments. This approach is being used to develop more effective treatments for mental health conditions.

- Digital mental health tools: There is a growing number of digital mental health tools available, such as apps, online programs, and wearable devices. These tools can help people to track their symptoms, learn coping skills, and connect with others who are facing similar challenges.

- Mental health awareness and stigma reduction: There is a growing awareness of the importance of mental health and well-being, and a growing movement to reduce stigma associated with mental illness. This is leading to greater acceptance and support for people with mental health conditions.

These trends and developments are making the future of mental health brighter. People with mental health conditions are living longer and healthier lives, and they have access to a wider range of effective treatments and support services.

Here are some specific ways in which the future of mental health could be even brighter:

- Increased investment in mental health research and treatment: Governments and funding agencies could invest more in mental health research and treatment. This would help to develop more effective treatments and make mental health services more accessible and affordable.

- Improved integration of mental health and physical health care: Mental health and physical health are closely linked, but they are often treated separately. In the future, mental health care and physical health care could be more integrated, so that people receive the holistic care they need.

- Greater focus on prevention: In the future, there could be a greater focus on preventing mental health problems from developing in the first place. This could involve promoting resilience and teaching people coping skills.

- Reduced stigma associated with mental illness: Stigma associated with mental illness is a major barrier to people seeking help. In the future, there could be a greater effort to reduce stigma and to create a more supportive and inclusive society for people with mental health conditions.

By investing in mental health research and treatment, integrating mental health and physical health care, focusing on prevention, and reducing stigma, we can create a brighter future for mental health.

CONCLUSION

Mental health is an important part of overall well-being. It is essential for our ability to live happy, fulfilling lives. However, mental health problems are common, and they can have a significant impact on our lives.

This book has provided an overview of mental health, including the different types of mental health problems, the causes of mental health problems, and the available treatments. It has also discussed the importance of mental health advocacy and the future of mental health.

If you are struggling with a mental health problem, it is important to know that you are not alone. There are many people who understand what you are going through, and there are many resources available to help you get the support you need.

Here are some specific things you can do if you are struggling with a mental health problem:

- Talk to a trusted friend or family member. They can offer support and advice.
- Seek professional help from a therapist or counsellor. They can help you to understand

your mental health problem and develop coping mechanisms.

- Join a support group. This can provide you with a safe space to connect with others who are facing similar challenges.

- Get involved in mental health advocacy. This can help you to make a difference in the lives of others and to create a more supportive society for people with mental health conditions.

Remember, you are not alone. There is help available, and you can get better.

The future of mental health is bright. With advances in research and treatment, people with mental health conditions are living longer and healthier lives. There is also a growing awareness of the importance of mental health and well-being, which is leading to greater acceptance and support for people with mental health conditions.

By working together, we can create a brighter future for mental health.

GLOSSARY

Term	Definition	Example
Affective disorders	A group of mental health conditions characterised by disturbances in mood. Examples include depression, bipolar disorder, mania, and cyclothymia.	A person with depression may experience persistent sadness, loss of interest in activities, changes in appetite and sleep, and feelings of worthlessness or guilt.
Anxiety disorders	A group of mental health conditions characterized by excessive fear, worry, and anxiety. Examples include generalized anxiety disorder (GAD), social anxiety disorder, phobias, and obsessive-	A person with generalised anxiety disorder (GAD) may worry excessively about a variety of things, such as work, health, and relationships. They may find it difficult to relax or feel at peace, and they may experience physical symptoms

	compulsive disorder (OCD).	such as muscle tension, fatigue, and headaches.

Term	Definition	Example
Cognitive behavioural therapy (CBT)	A type of psychotherapy that focuses on the relationship between thoughts, feelings, and behaviours. CBT helps individuals identify and change unhelpful thinking patterns and behaviours that contribute to their mental health problems.	A person with social anxiety disorder may work with a CBT therapist to identify and challenge negative thoughts about themselves and their interactions with others. They may also learn relaxation techniques to manage anxiety symptoms.
Depression	A common mental health disorder characterised by persistent sadness, loss of interest in activities,	A person with depression may withdraw from social activities, have difficulty concentrating at work or school, and struggle to

	changes in appetite and sleep, and feelings of worthlessness or guilt.	get out of bed in the morning. They may also have thoughts of death or suicide.

Term	Definition	Example
Generalised anxiety disorder (GAD)	A chronic anxiety disorder characterised by excessive worry about a variety of things.	A person with GAD may experience excessive worry about work, health, finances, relationships, or other aspects of their lives. They may also experience physical symptoms such as muscle tension, fatigue, headaches, and digestive problems.
Mental health	A state of well-being in which an individual realises his or her own abilities, can cope with the normal stresses of life, can work productively	A person with good mental health is able to manage stress, build relationships, and achieve their goals. They also have a positive outlook on life and feel

	and fruitfully, and is able to make a contribution to her or his community.	connected to others.

Term	Definition	Example
Mental health first aid	A course that teaches individuals how to help someone who is experiencing a mental health crisis or challenge.	A person who has completed mental health first aid training may be able to recognize the signs of a mental health crisis, such as suicidal thoughts or self-harming behaviours, and provide support to the individual until professional help arrives. They may also be able to de-escalate a situation and direct the individual to appropriate resources.

Term	Definition	Example
Mental illness	A condition that affects a person's thinking, feeling, or behaviour and may lead to distress and difficulty in functioning.	A person with a mental illness may experience symptoms such as hallucinations, delusions, obsessive-compulsive behaviours, or disorganised thinking and speech. These symptoms can interfere with their daily life, relationships, and ability to work or go to school.
Obsessive-compulsive disorder (OCD)	A mental health disorder characterised by intrusive thoughts (obsessions) and repetitive behaviours (compulsions) that are aimed at reducing	A person with OCD may have intrusive thoughts about contamination, danger, or symmetry. They may engage in compulsive behaviours such as excessive

	anxiety.	hand-washing, checking locks, or ordering or arranging objects in a specific way.

Term	Definition	Example
Panic disorder	A mental health disorder characterised by sudden and unexpected episodes of intense fear that are accompanied by physical symptoms such as a racing heart, sweating, and difficulty breathing.	A person with panic disorder may experience panic attacks that occur without warning. They may also live in fear of having another attack.
Post-traumatic stress disorder (PTSD)	A mental health disorder that can develop after experiencing or witnessing a traumatic event, such as war, natural disaster, or physical assault.	PTSD symptoms may include flashbacks, nightmares, avoidance of reminders of the trauma, and hypervigilance. A person with PTSD may experience flashbacks of the traumatic event, have difficulty

		sleeping, and feel constantly on guard. They may also avoid reminders of the trauma and become easily startled.
Term	**Definition**	**Example**
Psychosis	A condition in which a person loses contact with reality and experiences symptoms such as hallucinations (seeing or hearing things that are not there) and delusions (false beliefs).	A person with psychosis may also have difficulty thinking clearly, making decisions, and communicating with others. They may withdraw from social activities and become isolated.
Schizophrenia	A chronic mental health disorder characterised by delusions, hallucinations, and	A person with schizophrenia may experience delusions of grandeur, persecution, or control. They

| | disorganised thinking and speech. | may also hear voices or see things that are not there. Their speech may be disorganised, and their thoughts may be difficult to follow. |

Term	Definition	Example
Self-care	Activities that promote mental and physical well-being.	Examples of self-care activities include exercise, healthy eating, getting enough sleep, spending time with loved ones, engaging in hobbies, and practicing relaxation techniques such as yoga or meditation.
Stigma	Negative attitudes and beliefs about mental illness that can lead to discrimination and social isolation.	Stigma can prevent people from seeking help for mental health problems, and it can make it difficult for those with mental illness to live fulfilling lives.

Term	Definition	Example
Therapy	A general term for treatment that is provided by a mental health professional, such as a therapist or counsellor. Therapy can involve talking about one's thoughts and feelings, learning new coping skills, and taking medication.	Different types of therapy include cognitive behavioural therapy (CBT), dialectical behaviour therapy (DBT), psychodynamic therapy, and interpersonal therapy (IPT).
Treatment	The process of helping someone with a mental health disorder manage their symptoms and improve their quality of life.	Treatment for mental health disorders can include therapy, medication, and lifestyle changes. The specific type of treatment that is most effective will vary depending on the individual and

the disorder.

AFTERWORD

As you conclude your exploration of "Things You Should Know: Mental Health," I hope you have gained a deeper understanding of this multifaceted aspect of human well-being. Remember, mental health is not merely the absence of mental illness; it is a dynamic state of being that encompasses our emotional, psychological, and social well-being.

Throughout this journey, you have learned about the various dimensions of mental health, including the different types of mental health conditions, their causes, and the effective strategies for managing and treating them. You have also explored the importance of self-care, social connection, and seeking professional help when needed.

As you continue on your path to mental well-being, remember that you are not alone. Mental health challenges are prevalent, and there are numerous resources available to support you. Embrace the power of self-compassion, cultivate healthy coping mechanisms, and seek help when you need it.

Thank you for investing your time and energy in learning about mental health. Together, we can create a world where mental well-being is valued, supported, and celebrated.

Sincerely,

Alex Murphy

Printed in Great Britain
by Amazon

50422998R00066